What Little Kitten Wants

T0372660

by Kathryn Harper
illustrated by Paula Bowles

'Little Kitten wants to play,' said Min.

'Stop!' said Lee.

'Little Kitten doesn't like that.'

'Little Kitten wants to ride,' said Min.

'Stop!' said Lee.

'Little Kitten doesn't like that.'

'Little Kitten wants to wash,' said Min.

'Stop!' said Lee.

'Little Kitten doesn't like that.'

'Little Kitten wants to dress up,' said Min.

'Stop!' said Lee.
'Little Kitten doesn't like that.'

'Little Kitten wants to eat,' said Min.

'Stop!' said Lee.

'Little Kitten doesn't like that.'

'What does Little Kitten want?' said Min.

'Look,' said Lee.

'Little Kitten wants this.'

'Little Kitten wants to cuddle, too,' said Min.

'Yes!' said Lee.

What Little Kitten Wants ● Kathryn Harper

Teaching notes written by Sue Bodman and Glen Franklin

Using this book

Developing reading comprehension

Min thinks that she can play with Little Kitten like a toy. It takes big brother Lee to help Min appreciate that Little Kitten needs to be treated gently. Consistency of text presentation and some repetition of sentence patterns supports the reader to manage two to three lines of text on each page. The goal at this band is for the children to follow the print with their eyes, only rarely using finger-pointing at points of difficulty

Grammar and sentence structure

- The reporting clause appears within the dialogue.
- Punctuation supports phrased and expressive reading.
- Use of a simple contraction 'doesn't'.

Word meaning and spelling

- Opportunity to rehearse and recognise frequently occurring words in context – 'said', 'to', 'want', 'Stop'.
- Sound out simple words and blend phonemes from left to right.

Curriculum links

Science – Animals need to be looked after properly. They must be treated well, whether kept as pets or as part of farming. Choose a range of animals kept in the locality and make a chart of the things that they need.

PSHE – Develop posters showing how to look after a kitten well. Include playing with, feeding, exercising and playing with a kitten, adding a ✗ under the incorrect way and a ✓ under the correct way.

Learning Outcomes

Children can:

- use punctuation to inform phrasing and expression

- use phonic knowledge to solve new and novel words
- comment on the events and characters in the story, making links to other stories and non-fiction texts.

A guided reading lesson

Book Introduction

Give each child a book and read the title to them.

Orientation

Give a brief overview of the book, using the verb in the same form as it is in text. Say: Here is Min. She is taking Little Kitten for a ride. Do you think that Little Kitten wants to ride? Look at her face. I don't think she likes that. Let's find out.

Preparation

Page 2: Say: Min thinks that Little Kitten wants to play. Find the word that says 'Min'. Say it slowly to check you have the right word. Now find the words 'Little Kitten'.

Page 3: Min's brother Lee thinks that Little Kitten doesn't like that. Have a look at the pictures. What do you think? Yes, Little Kitten's face is not happy. Lee asks Min to stop. Find the word 'stop'. Say it slowly.

Page 4: What does Min think Little Kitten wants now? Let's check if you are right. Let's read together. 'Little Kitten wants to –'. Get your mouth ready to say it. Do you think 'ride' would fit there? Does it look right? Yes, it says 'ride'.

Page 5: What does Lee think about it? Yes, Lee knows that Little Kitten doesn't like that. Let's practise reading what Lee says. Rehearse reading the text on page 5.

Repeat on pages 8 and 10.

Pages 6 to 11: Ask the children to look through the pages to see what else Min thinks that Little Kitten wants. Discuss to ensure that the vocabulary is familiar to them.